# A Long Late Pledge

# A Long Late Pledge

## WENDY WILLIS

*poems*

BEAR STAR PRESS

A LONG LATE PLEDGE

Please direct inquiries here:
BEAR STAR PRESS
www.bearstarpress.com
185 Hollow Oak Drive
Cohasset, CA 95973


Cover photograph by Gina Soden: www.ginasoden.co.uk
Book design by Beth Spencer


ISBN: 978-0-9850584-8-7
Library of Congress Control Number:  2017938908




Thanks to Dorothy Brunsman
for her support through the years.

*for Coy Leathers, my grandfather—*
*may he be beloved by my daughters and our descendants*
*to the thousandth and thousandth generation*

*Come now, close. And hush.*
*It's a long river back. A cruel river—*
*Back.*

*It's a taut neck, a trek.*
*A snake—its back.*
*A river's black walk.*

*A stitch and a stroke.*
*A bare-knuckled crank.*
*A snake-bit crawl.*

*A push off, a push over—*
*All to conjure dark.*
*Even the stars' cold scars—*

*Broken and harsh. Hush.*
*Recall. Recoil.*
*A secret's first secret: Where.*

*Then, why. To bevy too close*
*To mud-sunk truth, to scrape deep—*
*Skin, then tendon, then bone.*

*Then come close. Then come back.*
*Then come home.*

# TABLE OF CONTENTS

A Tatted Script

More Perfect Union

## ANCIENT LIBERTIES & FREE CUSTOMS

# A Long Late Pledge

# A Tatted Script

*Tat*:

1) the act or process of using a shuttle to knot cotton or linen lace

2) slang for tattoo

## Dear DAR, an Essay

What can I say now to un-name the nation?
Should I sketch the ridge of second growth,

glinty and jagged as a wolf's mouth? Or recount
the cabman's wrists, small and dark as my own,

his coffee-stained belly pressed to the wheel?
What shall I recall of the Capitol—firefly-shiny

and intertwined—or of the old-country dumplings
boiled for memory's sake? Is it too late to seize

the tatted script before it wears threadbare,
my mind thin as my grandmother's one good cup?

I know there's no time now to resuscitate the reputation
of the Russians or the raccoon struck twice by lightning.

There's no need to call forth a Chicago sunrise
of spiky streets and industry. No.

You would despise the books that led me here—
open and close your cracking lips, suck on the secrets

in the back of your throat. You would let the last door slam.
What can I say to un-name this blue and bloodied land?

# On Dreaming Mr. Jefferson Riding Home to Monticello

Even at dawn I know. It will only be once. Just this once
though I am witched. Witched with waiting and wanting,
bending low for the shattering of hooves. Curved,
straining. Down-curved, bent like a water witch. Strained
for the clatter of hooves, for a whiff of the sea. Passing down
curve & strain, passing down knowing, passing down want.

≈

That day, this day, the day I dreamt the squirrel hunt. The forest bristling
and restless with late leaves, the sky so flat it tastes like shale.
It splinters like shale, it lasts like chalk. The men come back squirreled

and singing fire. For me, it's all sapling-boned loss and want for the sea.
A hand on an iron pot, a hunt at the spring, firewood dropped at the sight:
Red and cruel with the whip. Wordless & narrow-eyed & rattling,

the horse bolting hard and bare, its bay red shoulder strained to break.
Breakneck, break away, heartbreak, halfway. Brake. And broke
& me left cracked. Me, not yet quicked but cracked and left

sniffing like a wolf:  sea salt, tobacco & half-rotted apples, brine
& full-rotted nets. Clinging to Him like ground fog. A pocket
of crabapple seeds, a low song for an elk. A moan for a lost lover,

cold and open mouthed—a full-scale want, a half-turned want.
But none of it a hardness. The cruelty of now but none of it hard.
Though want bellows like an elk and reeks like a marsh,

wishing turns want to salt. Wanting what is gone, what has never been:
Paris, the Capitol, the Tidewater. A bull elk. A great and pacific West.
The passing down of want is swallowing a lightning bug. It is nipples,

hard and raw against rough-spun muslin. Untouched, untouchable.
Groping for oysters and the wet salt sea. No, not the Tidewater.
Yes, a great and pacific West. A freshwater river running to a saltwater sea.

## On First Encountering Lightning Bugs Near the Tidal Basin

I did not know night could come on that hot,
limp and languid as a blanket in a bathtub.

I want to say my mother held my hand
though it is unlikely despite desire's

spiraling fractals. I want to say I heard the cicadas'
triumphant return, though that is unlikely

except in the songs of the lucky, which I am not.
I want to say I conjured you whole,

bronzed and backlit from the dark portico
on the white beach.

Though we both know that is the flattest of lies.
Instead, I will leave you this:

your mind is a ravenous fog
laying claim to every spare acre.

## They Say It Makes Us Strong to Swim Before Winter's End
### swim lesson, Springfield

Don't they smell the way the dark still clings to day,
keeping us moldering and mute? It's March
1973 and later I'll learn that John Dean is warning
about a cancer on the presidency. He had no idea.
But I am still pressed up under the Doug fir,
nipping at the mist. I close my eyes and hear
the swim bus engine knock knock knock
like a prisoner. The steam on the windows
drapes a curtain of damp over damp,
a canvas for finger-drawn hearts, for *BK + LM*,
for a crooked and underlined *shit*
just above the aluminum lip.

To dispatch, the driver:
*It's running rich. Or dry. Or something.*

Me: *I didn't know rich & dry were opposites.*

## WATERGATE

I still don't dare name the bend in the road
where I first heard the word, the one trembling
like a tuning fork, like a nosebleed.

Fir chips piled high as the gritty foothills,
smoldering with ruffles, chuffing with shame.
Our mothers rattle stiff muslin drapes

across all that is bright or blue. And even so,
I hear the radio news man draw his first sharp breath.
Slick with the alphabet of the dumb,

my mind fissures with mirthlessness,
spun glassy with words passing by but not through:
pelican, Port au Prince, plasma, platypus

lipids, listeria, lassitude, lord of the dance said he
gangrene, gladiola, graciousness, glyphs
willowbark, wisteria, wanderlust, woe.

And just like that, I recall last summer's sparrow
cupped in my two brittle hands.
A flittering in the chest, a stone in the throat.

An instant pricked like the tip of a pin
shimmering between the fluttered loss of open palms
and the shattering press of prayer.

## Doctrine of Discovery: Notes on the State of America
*for TJ*

It's still too cool for June and high time to lie low
and call forth the auspices of this *terra nullius*,
this land of blue-backed crows and black-capped
chickadees, this land of ex-trappers & ex-loggers,
ex-fisher-ex-convicts & excommunicated explorers.

It'll take a long look at the auguries of this land
is your land, my land, this land of landfall, land-lust,
landlocked longing. This gristle-damp land, this land
of elk-hide and holdouts. Yes, it's high time to account
for assimilation & assignations, late arrivals & early blights,

at least at this long-shadowed latitude—45 degrees North.
Out here in Mr. Jefferson's garden of the world.

~

It only took a dust bowl, a half-term of Old Hickory
and two generations to leave us
tallying blood quantum and burrowing for air.

These days, ink-tongued crows shake out
the morning like a picnic blanket. And us? We're still restless
& squawking, trying to glue the pieces together

like a box of mismatched saucers
shattered in a cross-country move.
And here I am. One foot—as they say—in each camp.

Thanks to M'Intosh and the Illinois & Wabash,
there's a red wax string running from Shadwell
straight to the mouth of the Columbia.

~

I wonder what it would have been like if I'd thrown
my lot in with the furriers or the Finns canning salmon,
tossing innards—bloody & iron-soaked—back

to the circling gulls. Nothing a steam bath and a nip
of gin couldn't solve. Listen, I can't pretend
to be a woman who will settle for a songbird.

From here, I'll take a belt & suspenders approach:

But now I've got a thief's title to this tiny lot
in this great big state. I've turned over my shovel,
raised my flag. Now, one hand's guarding my purse
and the other's finger-counting the hours.

English peas sprout in March, but it's never hot
enough here for melons. Keep a weather eye
for blossom rot & early blight. As for you,
you stirred up consternation in Lynchburg by eating

a tomato—whole—right in the public square.
Yes, you can call this the New World now.

~

Per J. Adams:
*But Mr. Jefferson tells large stories.*

~

Last fall, the Greek woman in Montgomery County:
*Honey, are you a Melungeon?*

Must be why I can't help but sniff for smoke
beyond that next, shimmery ridge.

I should suppose it's a blessing
to be taken for whatever bird-boned settler wanders in.

My sister, though, she's a looker. Stone straight hair to her waist
and eyes as near to blue as anything else.

But the shovel teeth & diabetes to prove it.
My weaknesses tend to run toward the bottle.

But it's all half-stories anyway.
Nothing near as certain as your Niña, your Pinta, your Santa Maria.

~

And perchance, *The Doctrine of Discovery*—

Though the clouds were full and threatening war,
we planted our wingless flag on a windless moon,
landing those moonwalkers pie-eyed & dry.
Now the Russians rush to flag the northern sea,
leaving little elbow room for the great blue whale

and the blessed rest of us.

~

I will pass down to the thousandth and thousandth generation:

The Northwest Passage, in reverse.
Down river first, broad & motherish, effluvial & rich.

A fertile and handsome valley. A compass pointing only West.
Aquaphobia, ophidiophobia. A ghost elk, silver-hided & stalky.
An owl—its hollow whoosh, lightless and colorless and needleless.
A net for blackcaps, a swath of starlings haunting the dump.
A wolf by the ear & a stirring certainty.
Late summer dripping with coiled snakes & loathing.

~

I have several other skills, not many of them useful.

I can declaim the Presidents in reverse order and have sketched
the gowns of the first ladies. Under no circumstances can I guess
the weight of a smelt. I can whistle the theme song for *Bonanza*.
First God, then boys, then supper. The only French
my little daughter can recall is *oeuf*. But the 10 chosen woodsmen
didn't know a lick and got by with tin medals and stolen canoes.
I have heard a forest fire throw its voice like a nighthawk.
I know how to paint by numbers. A mumbled amen. A half-forgotten
we-the-people. I could have married a logger but did not.
I pack a pair of scissors and a solid roll of tape.

*Yes*, I snap back.
As Lady Thatcher used to say, *most of us die washing cups*.

~

In the end, my one, I still can't stand the Federalists.

Yet I stay here
in God's half-acre where the commonweal is tame & flaccid,
where ghost trees shimmer when the city's peeled back,
where babies are named *Anchors Away* and the war is less picturesque.
I'll rely on my tin ear & sharp tongue.
I'll carry the keys. You said *the dead are not even things.*
And yet extinction—despite your prediction—has its rewards.

~

God bless you.
And God bless the United States of America.

## ARS DEMOCRACIA

Who am I to wield this pen from the provinces?
To wind and unwind America's purled promises—
shuttle in one hand, splitting maul in the other?

Who am I to topstitch hither to yon?
To name drop, name names, natter on, normalize
for nativists, swallow what is noxious and what is not?

I, who have not been elected by virtue of one man,
one vote or appointed and confirmed by the Senate.
Not even convicted by a jury of my peers.

I am neither aristocracy nor intelligentsia though I am covetous
like both. I am yeoman & fishwife. I am taxidermist & tailor,
indebted to soothsayers & oracles though recognized by none.

And what would the Chief Justice say if I confessed?
If I cracked under oath: *I pried these words from under the tongues*
*of great black birds, then issued the order—*

*Devour them.* If I declared:  *It was I. I, whose only sworn witness*
*is the cold moon. The sole testimony on matters of both church and state.*
No. I am neither certified nor ordained to chuff my singed breath

into the powdered curls at the back of your neck.
To swoon at the sound of your name. To revere and lollygag,
to invoke Article II, section 1. I know it will be said that I stole

the pen, the maul, the blood-red thread. That I slithered in
uninvited, between the deserving and the descended.
Yes, my memory is looped & addled. But it is no worse

than that of the Chinook, swim-spent but still bashing
its hooked head against Mr. Roosevelt's dams, or the geese
that forget to fly south and now circle in an insatiable storm.

It is no secret that I have carnal knowledge of the overripe world,
soft and split like the last plum left for rain. I am adept at jealousy
and the kitchener stitch. I am a righteous descendent of peasant

& bastard & Indian. I know the likes of me will never be called
to stroke your bedclothes or guard your tin spectacles.
Though I am too common to carry the torch, I am the one

who—sleepless and alone—listens to the wind
take issue with the trees, who witnesses the triumph
of the seditious dawn, then hears the sky whimper & shift.

Oddling that I am, yes, I am the one. I am the one kneeling in ink,
gawking, hoping & hopeless; mumbling & rasping
but near certain the Republic will lurch on.  My lips to God's ear.

## STITCH: THE FOREST

The forest is coy year after year,
until the day it lifts its sharp skirt
for the licking flame. The winds
hiss their *tsk tsk*s. What is it
they would have me mend?
(Purse-string sutures are shaky but painless.)
When the fates shout down the heresy of stitch,
I can't help but turn to the nurse log,

to the unravel of the blood line,
to the tear from sea to (shining) sea.
Like a seam gone bad, black flies and maggots set in.
Trains, with their midnight horns,
pass just beneath the skin.
My companions are quotidian. A sampler of loss.

# MORE PERFECT UNION

*The government of a family, bears a Lilliputian resemblance to a nation.*
—Mary Randolph in *The Virginia Housewife: Or, Methodical Cook*

## We the People: A Genealogy

And this is the book of the generations of the sassafras,
which, with its mitten-handed leaves and pepper-sweet
skin, must not be far back in the book of the begats.

And the sassafras begat Adam back before apple
& snake. And Adam begat Seth & Cain
& Enoch. And one of them passed down a hand for the whip

because one of those fine men who lived to nine hundred
& five, he begat our own land's fathers with fists formed
for the handle. But then I was begat & begat

another and where will end the book of my begats?
I curl under the shade of Grandmother Sassafras,
for surely she is a she, and me round & sticky

as the butterscotched sun, I know this—
I begat the one with a backbone of sugar.
I will pass along a fear of the milk snake & a taste

for bitter song. I will not begat the breath to swim
or a shoulder for the plow. But I will pass a thin heart,
my one and only name. And this land will bear sons,

but most certainly there will be daughters.

## STITCH: AN ANNUNCIATION

*Coarse as a horsetail,*
Mother chuffs as she brushes
ninety-nine strokes

with a boar bristle brush,
spit & tug, plaits
flat as dinner plates.

My mind turns up blank.
It's true. I cannot spin for the life of me.
But I knit cruel whispers off the wind.

So when that sun-dazzled he leans
out of his late autumn halo
and twists a slipped strand

between forefinger and thumb,
the day bursts as a beehive,
the pumpkins sweeten in the field.

## ARROWS OF DESIRE: A MELANCHOLY

One year—between kisses—
we rolled out our dead
between us,
like so many shriveled walnuts.
We cracked them open
and called them by name:
lamprey & wire cutter & tongue coral.
This year, between silences,

you recite Blake's *Jerusalem*.
I knit the codicils of the *Magna Carta*.
Despite the late hour, I still can't recall
the name for pomegranate.
I search my mind for temptation.
A persimmon rolls out of my mouth.

## Staining the Sky with Wings

Last night I dreamt a bottle tree,
the split hickory
at the bottom of the drive—
heart-shaped & rattling & glittered.
I crept down the copper-dust road,
the sassafras smelling sweet
as new death or rum.
The wind lifted.
A cloud of grackles
quick with a squall,
staining the sky with cobalt & bronze,
staining the sky with wings.

~

They say it marks a bearing woman's child
if she looks upon a snake
or an open grave.
But listen, this child is already marked.

Marked with the coin eyes of my father,
tobacco colored & thick lidded.
Marked with my mother's rabbit heart
and the sea-salt smell of love.

She's marked with a restless foot
and a backbone of sugar.
But that's not what they mean.
They mean death greets a woman

with a pick & a spade.
They mean death coils in the rocks
and strikes the unsuspecting.
And maybe they are right.

For this child is most certainly already marked.
As are we all.

～

They'll say I bore the child
of the summer sky.
They'll say I swallowed the clouds,

cottony & vague & wisped. But it is not the clouds
I swallow:  it is the grackle song—
restless & inky. Restless & blank.

I swallow the quick tail
of the corn snake, coiled
tight as the fist of a foundling.

I swallow the cruel rider's whip.
I swallow wasps pressing paper
in the barn. I swallow sparks

from the dark judge's gavel.
And pantry moths
& witch bottles & heat lightning.

I swallow the molasses
of the blind preacher's gospel
and the hot prick of a lightning bug.

I swallow the last jagged hour
of the dog star, the new moon's crease.
I swallow the owl's swift call. Yes,

I swallow the night.

## Stitch: My Throat

My throat is full of morning glory.
Flossy, irreverent, aching to breed.

My lungs are full of late summer nasturtiums.
My veins are full of prime numerals.

Cause of death: strangulation
By nasturtium, by morning glory,

By 11 & 19.
By late summer grief, by nasturtium

By morning glory. Cause of death:
Strangulation.

My veins are full of prime numerals.
My chest is full of late nasturtiums.

Flossy, irreverent, aching to breed.
My throat is full of morning glory.

## STITCH: A WARNING

Oh, deer heart, russet heart,
peeling-velvet heart,

sleek and ferny heart,
candle-wicking deer heart,

dear heart,
rise slow.

Sniff the last wisp of warning
off the wind.

If I should not outlive the brackish dark,
bury my tatted, knitted,

whipped & stitched,
nearly mended heart

beneath a mossy log
—moldering—

far from the sun.

## Compulsory Education

There is something gentle about a lintel,
the word worn and soft as unwashed sheets.
Nothing like the steel of a helicopter blade

or a coffin nail hammered to keep witches at bay.
Loftier than a threshold with its scabbed
bitterness and unmarked lust

for the quivering first days of autumn.
And yet I do not want those daughters of mine
entering the world under such a thing

suspended by some untestable law
of physics & faith. God bless the separation
of church & state. Maybe just a few moments

more here in the hall. Behind a forbidding shield
of cobwebby windows
(it's a live and let live arrangement around here).

I say: *I can't stop thinking of the meteorite in Central Park West.*
After rocketing between ice floes and greedy farmers,
it's come to rest. Now and then its people fly

east to wipe it with rosehip water
and a buffing cloth. Weighty as a chrysalis,
patient as a dying dog. Yes, I wish

I had invented the elevator shaft, had painted
St. Andrew's Cross, had blasted rank guitar

at tin pot dictators. But silence drifts. And soon
it'll be a snappy wave from the front porch,
the heart shrinking back toward the spine
hooded behind a screen of gristle & rib.

# Writ of Habeas Corpus

Love in this Republic has small habits,
rising like yeast in mid-summer,
spreading red

from the tip of a tent needle.
But I know enough to ask—
is prophecy more conjure or conjecture?

Answer slow.
The wind is a well-trained dog.
The sunset is the work of a thief.

The price of liberty is the color of algae,
and the earth stops turning in the hour
between dishes and pie.

Even houseguests avert their eyes.
The kitchen throws off its own weather,
hovering between tenderness

and complaint.
Now, my indiscretions tend
toward the botanical. Hothouse and florid,

wicked but too fragile for cross-examination.
I know the key is buried in a shallow pit.
Once I saw a photograph of a wounded rabbit,

a lethal plastic cone over its tiny, wild face,
the dark mercy of a hairless, murmuring beast—
no wind off the river, no grass underfoot.

# LETTER ON THE MATTER OF AN ELK FOR MONTICELLO

You should know there's a bull elk at 79th & Central Park West.
Head dipped, teeth bared to bellow, but frozen silent
He's parked just off the Teddy Roosevelt Room,

surrounded by cows—muscular & dusky & confused;
close by the Mandan village and the Clatsop canoes,
buzzing with yellow light and near-drowned in resin.

I understand you coveted an elk for the Grove at Monticello, a king
to reign over crabapples & chinaberries. And I know what you mean.
All last summer I stalked my own. Awake before dawn,

slinking low in the stumps and barely breathing, but like you,
no luck. You know, the Expedition you sent out to my corner
of the Republic killed one hundred thirty-one in just one winter.

For blankets and tallow and rancid meat. The place still tastes wet,
rotted, elky. And you with your six-point rack right in the front hall,
preening for the visit from Captain Lewis and the Mandan chief.

And what gets me, TJ, for all our yearning, TR has one all to himself.
He who guarded the continent against becoming *a game preserve*
*for squalid savages.* Each year, five million souls see the elk in Central Park.

I'm not sure who looks upon the Mandans. Last fall near home, a buck-shot elk
crashed the front gates of the zoo. Strawberry-stain wound on one flank
and eyes rolling like a spooked horse. Velvet peeling from antlers

in long, ringleted strips. Clattering bricks, he leapt into the mountain goat pen.
He lay down on his side, snorting steam and shattering the morning
with his bellows. Calling for comfort from the nearest hooved thing.

## BEAR HUNGRY

Is all I can think to call it, all ache and rankness.
It's been at least three years since I glimpsed one live.
But I saw a C-17, fat & gray & obliterate.
And then another (and another) until it was sometimes four an hour.

It's been at least three years since I glimpsed one live,
gray carrion carrying men sixteen across from here to Lord knows.
And then another (and another) until it was sometimes four an hour.
Now, the Canada geese stay north and settle the Indian school ball field.

Gray carrion carrying men sixteen across from here to Lord knows
where. The black bears scrabble the clearcut, shinnying and scratching,
but the Canada geese stay north and settle the Indian school ball field
near my garden where the old dog sleeps and chases his blue shadow.

While black bears scrabble the clearcut, shinnying and scratching,
the gray wolf and the grizzly are nothing but glittered ghosts.
In my garden, the old dog sleeps and chases her blue shadow,
long gone and still longing for an untamed heart.

The gray wolf and the grizzly are nothing but glittered ghosts,
but I saw a C-17, fat & gray & obliterate.
Long gone and still longing for an untamed heart.
Bare. Hungry. Is all I can think to call it. All ache and rankness.

## Stitch: The Street

The street off the porch is frayed
and puckering—opinionated in its antiquity.
I know I could free it with one great rip,
but I stop to listen for the nighthawks,
knowing they will do what they are given to do—
whistle & dive, pray & curse the dawn.
All the while I bunker down,
sip weak tea & fuss over the passing of the hours.

Then I stand, waving the children down the road,
one hand on my heart like a halfwit or a widow
straining to catch some half-remembered anthem.
In truth, it's not fealty but fear. The heart unravels
in the long run. The mind hangs on
by one tender and insatiable thread.

## Stitch: Hammond B

I can barely keep up with the news,
noting the notations, annotating the annotations,
calling roll for the last reluctant mammals.
Even the Hammond B will be held
to account in the tally of usefulness.
So far I can report only this: all the best lamentations
are sung right to left. The ions are anxious
in their losses yet boastful in their gains.

Current disputations dissolve into epigraphs
and tears. Now, the drapes of uncertainty hang
heavy & frayed. The hours slink by,
scolding me for timidity. Yes, I admit,
the vessel is weak but the wine is strong.
An oligarch walks into a bar.

# Ancient Liberties & Free Customs

*Plainly the sheep and the wolf are not agreed upon a definition of the word liberty . . .*

—Abraham Lincoln

## Saturday Night at Mary Todd's Workers Bar & Grill

In the way that such things begin—

A poet walks into a bar in search of America.
Sniffing for flag-soaked bromides & a whiff

of the Wobblies, for one last draught of cockfights
& want ads. For a doughnut philosopher, a breadline

optimist. But the longshoremen are long missing,
and the bar is slumped with a fiddler, a painter,

and a postman who sings in code. Not even a quarter-mile
off the purse-proud wharf and the only right answer is this:

*Looking for work.* Oh citizens of industry, praise be!
The poet arrives in time for the declamations & gnashing of teeth:

Recall the Benedictines!  *To labor is to pray!*
Then they pass the baby Jesus hand to hand.

The painter whispers: *Memento Mori.* As if He could forget.
The others coo back—*no, no, it's Semper Fi.*

A hobbled witness now, the poet sits and knits
alongside her clacking mind, nursing her fealty to the nation.

The tenderness of the word *coaxed* shatters her resolve.
And under her breath: *I seem to be the scapegoat for both*

*drizzle & drought.* She turns her ear toward the night-
black river, her tongue toward the deadly sea.

# ODDLING

This patch of grass is my ancient responsibility,
Ceded along with the white peaks

Of hither & yon. Hush now.
Please turn to one with a steadier hand.

I am unfamiliar with the gospel of lawn.
Ask a dull wife, a gay sky.

There is no solace in engraving my skin
With type, each bar and curve staking

Its own claim. I cannot complete a cuff,
Set a shoulder. My innards are full of arsenic,

Pickled and left on the sill.
But what can be knit by a sentinel?

As for your tally, go ahead now,
Mark both theft & abandonment.

## Trade Negotiations

The neighbor, in her listless kindness,
offers me a choice
between a henhouse, a boulder, and a saw mill.

The trade-offs are clear and imminent
(she must be running for higher office).
*Valencia*, I stall, *an orange so singular,*

*it is a metaphor for itself.*
*It could be a personality test*
*or a prank for a television pilot.*

The furnace is already in poor repair.
*What about spun sugar? What about cut glass?*
*Flat and white,* she replies. *There is no currency in allusions.*

The boulder is tempting as they are rarely seen
in these parts, at least not whole and up close.
And everyone knows, it has cracked the code—

waiting out dictators, trading cigars in the cloakroom
of the Senate. It might right the tilt of the earth.
But I am unused to intimacy with objects

of such magnitude. Not wishing to seem ungrateful,
*What about a mango grove? An evening gown?*
*A disco ball? What about a tug boat?*

She: *You've always been jealous of the fowl.*
Retort: *It's all a mammalian misunderstanding anyhow.*
What does the backside of my brain have to say?

(Sleep, sleep, sleep)
The trade-offs are clear but not imminent.
Mussels, with their bearded hearts

are as sure as anything I've ever reveled in.
But salmon roe bears nothing
except heartache. In our dithering

we are neglecting the electorate
and the budding lawn.
A saw mill sounds more noble

than a pulp mill. But either way,
too much churning between labor and industry.
It would be un-Christian to reverse progress.

*What about a paddle wheel? A clothesline?*
*What about a sapphire ring? A Venus flytrap?*
*That's enough*, she snaps. *I know the coyote skims*

*close at night.* Meekly: *A blueberry blossom?*
Truth be told, even an egg is beyond my control.
It ends up tipping like a three-wheeled pram and the press

does its scrabbling anyway. Always the life of the party.
And this is no time to bring hatchlings around the House,
mighty and mewling, the color of variegated marigolds,

the smell of cocktail hour. And yet it is the henhouse
that stirs patriotism abroad. I would have been happy curled
into myself, wrists folded like a paper crane.

For now my eggs are made of wool and spun cotton.
They seem safer, tamer, less likely to catch fire.
Is this what it means to become beatific?

In the heroics of my hamstrung mind, I rummage like a wild boar—
stout and four-chinned, but I am unpracticed in both poker
and braggadocio. The trade-offs are neither imminent nor clear.

I could close my eyes and acquaint myself with the boulder.
The neighbor, in her jackrabbit lassitude, rescinds her final offer.
It all runs together now. *Whatever became of taxation without representation?*

## STITCH: THE NEEDLE

The needle of the Republic is stored in an undisclosed location.
Waiting for the reprieve of horsehair and flax.
There will be no parade, but the bonfire issues
its own invitations, calls in its own debts.
The summer was as blistered as we deserved,
and oh how we squandered the long light
on handwringing and coat-tails.
Now my basket overflows in brokenness.

With my needle of disreputable origin, there is anguish
to be mended but also breakfast dishes & depositions.
Believe me, the temptation is strong to baste the tongue.
Muteness would be a solace now. Yes, I know
what they say: *This is the woman who unravels the blankets of the dead.*
Blessedly, my hand is steady, but my sight is dim.

## INK & NEEDLE OF A COMPASS ROSE

*The soothsayers, magicians, prophets, & princes of old would think us as errant fools as we think them knaves.*

—John Ledyard to Thomas Jefferson, July 5, 1788

Let me tell it to you straight.

I know all about that boy, the one you met, wild-eyed and wet, inherited in Paris.
How you seduced him with your full-moon mind and your glittery talk
of walking across the Bering Sea like some kind of West-wandering Christ.

*All it takes*, you told him, *is an English foot, two sharp sticks and a circled dragged
in the dust. To discern latitude and the nation's width.* You dashed that foot—blue &
cruel into the tender, vein-rivered flesh of his forearm. Twelve inches

from lash to lash, then passed him the darning needle—new British steel—
& a sharpening flint. Tempted him to mark his way home, jot notes
in berry juice & charcoal, ink into the skin of his mother's son.

∼

And what is it you would have of me, my barrister—my banisher—
now that I'm cast out here on the edge? The clouds are too thick to steer

by stars and there's no hope for a jeweled bearing. Out here in Clark's half-acre
without a mark or a stick, how shall I keep track of this mossy empire?

Latitude on the back of the neck—45 degrees north—the white wisp
of a waxwing's tail, a fistful of beads amongst women?

Between the thighs, valleys inked with childbirth & fear? A recipe
for strawberry jelly on the elbow, the directions for a poultice behind the knee?

Would you see that on the round of my haunch is a new moon, *Federalist 10*,
*Song of Myself*? Would you know of the severed heart in the small of my back?

∾

And what do we have for marking? There are blueberries
for Fourth of July. And huckleberries through September.
Thimbleberries and blackberries fill every clear space,

but the marionberries are to be saved for pie. In November,
there will be cranberries floating in the bog. And currants
and crab apples on hand. Even so, there are stitches to consider.

It only takes one gold-eyed needle & a hank of silken floss,
top-stitching the road home into my half-red skin. If the strawberries
are too hard & seedy: a darning needle, a crewel needle, an awl.

∾

Even in these times, I hear whispers of a mermaid,
heavy fleshed and fine boned,

kin to sturgeon. And still my skin is the color of silt,
not early but late—

one stroke farther up the cold river,
one stroke farther from the bay.

∾

I've sailed over that river bar only once—
it spilling hard and countless like that which is not to be mentioned
in mixed company—full of lamprey and farm-bred

salmon. Anyway, I only went once.
With a boatload of lawyers, a stripper in the hold
& a Korean boy who called me *Magnolia*

when the waters ran rough. But I kissed him anyway
and let him stand on the top step. I like a man
whose diaspora runs in a straight line.

⮴

And yet in these hours of unceasing prayer, there are honeybees
to finger count & Coho fry to tally. The sea otters have gone,

and I have laid eyes on a beaver only once. I have learned
to flush elk from the dusk; I have a broody hen penned

beneath my clavicle. I've heard tell of a bearing black badger & scores
of western chub. The cutthroat & steelhead & lamprey are making due.

I've seen a Clark's nuthatch and a black-billed magpie. The mammoths
—even you must give over—never were. The cormorant & coyote

& common crow have found their way and are in no need of a dispatch.
Above my right ear, the price of corn; my left, the health of the family

farm: *poor.* I ceaselessly rack up gossip—*adulteress, wanderer,*
and there is breakfast & afterbirth to consider. My liver is etched

with your fine French wine, and if I find a cure for migraines,
I'll sketch it on my temple for you. The instruments are these:

threshing needle, canvas needle, embroidery number two.
Knitting needles dug up from the sand & a crochet hook

for curves. I cannot shake my fear of water, and I seem to need
my sacraments in twos. The distance between the border

and the Capitol is a long way off now. Not even an English foot
and a stick can get me there intact. And what news of the hearth?

I can tell you only this: Pregnant clouds linger, even into summer now.
The market is a great and insatiable beast. The citizenry is dazzled

& weak, but the Chinook still run in spring. I offer you this in dispatches
of ripe fruit & hard facts. Not many of them good. Remember that storm

of despotism? We know its shadow well. And there's this, my beloved
declarer of self-evidence: *maybe we are just not up to it.* And why

would we be—out here in the dark, where the hawks squall high
and the trees press higher, where we rarely see the sun? Why

would we be since we're settled into stolen lands with our eyes
stitched shut? My ankles, encircled with the twin serpents of wander

& sit. Lest you forget, I am lover, mother, sister-at-arms, citizen
of your great and Pacific West. And what good does it do you now?

My boots bring red dust right into your parlor, half-loved, half-breed,
& exhausted. But my lips are marked with multitudes. With gratitude

& fear. With the tremor of the trade winds and the skipping songs of children.
My lips are marked with rain. There's a palimpsest across my forehead—

nubilous days in Paris, slate skies of the Piedmont. No pineapples
here or pomegranates. Only uncertainty and grief. But there is the promise

of blackberries this summer. Tapioca for thickening.
And a pie crust in the pantry. The clouds are swollen forth to burst.

∾

This is it, my beloved. My scribe, you can rest here.
Reverse this ravishment of sands. Trace your stick in a circle

and mark the way home. Come close. See the slough
slide along the curve of my belly. Gray's Bay. Cape Disappointment.

This is the land where the river turns its back on the sea.

## A Long-Late Pledge

It's about time that I swear allegiance to this Republic
though I suppose those Washington counting men
have long counted me as one of their own. But I crossed

my fingers behind my back, mouthed the words,
sang *watermelon* under my breath. Now, there's no hope in waiting,
and here I am shaky and tired. But that's about right in this nation

where everybody looks rattled and shaken and tired. I understand
the shaken or shaky or shook up, but why for the love of God
and this good declaration is everyone so tired?

Owl-eyed and slow-flanked and tired. It must be the lights,
day and night, the lights. Have you ever seen those space-shots
of earth? So bright. Even dark is light. But I'd best raise my hand now

before the sun breaks its arc, before I break free, before I lose heart.

～

### I pledge allegiance

*supposing this nation needs the allegiance of shaky-kneed women, small owls,
cracked leather, cracked lips, cracked minds, nurse logs and huckleberry not yet ripe,
beak moss and cork boots, foxes long gone but whose spirits still nibble at fiddleheads,
late-day fog, spike prongs and clearcuts and redsides, loggers and lawyers, wild straw-
berry and wild mint, supposing this nation needs this sworn allegiance, supposing
this nation needs allegiance at all*

# TO THE FLAG

*they say there are two million stitches in a flag, must be twice that many*
*to keep that flag on the moon. four million tiny stitches. all sewn by hand*

## OF THE UNITED STATES OF AMERICA

*oh sing—this broken promise, this broken nation, this broken land—sing it back to whole*

## AND TO THE REPUBLIC FOR WHICH IT STANDS

*Mr. Lincoln tells it best:*

*It is for us the living, rather, to be dedicated here to the unfinished work. . . .*
*It is rather for us to be here dedicated to the great task remaining . . .*
*we take increased devotion to that cause for which they gave*
*the last full measure . . . we here highly resolve that these dead*
*shall not have died in vain—that this nation under God*
*shall have a new birth of freedom, and that government*
*of the people,*
*by the people,*
*for the people,*
*shall not perish from the earth*

## ONE NATION, UNDER GOD

*(and maybe that mighty God stashed a secret from the shattered rest of us)*

## INDIVISIBLE

*Ikenick Creek to Clear Lake to the McKenzie River over Cougar Dam past Finn*
*Rock and Nimrod to the confluence with the Willamette to the Main Stem picking*
*up Clackamas and Tualatin flowing north over Willamette Falls past Willamette*
*Baseline to the Columbia at Sauvie Island, Willamette on one side, Columbia on the*

*other, wider and faster and through Astoria with its tall ships*—Ocian in View!  O!
the Joy!—*the dark and merciless Pacific*

WITH LIBERTY AND JUSTICE FOR ALL.

It's going to take a lot more than a moose this time
to convince the French that this country
isn't withered & rife with noxious vapors.

The Republic's going to hell in a hand basket.
All the poets say so. Though on second thought,
a moose might not be a bad start. What with that high-speed train

and all, let's take him live this time. And forget about the French.
Let's walk him right through the front doors of the House
of Representatives. Knock. Like we're showing up

for the State of the Union. Antlers swinging, hooves skidding
marble. Seven feet tall. *Behold!* Of course then there'll be a debate
between Alaska and Wyoming on the origins of this moose.

And the South Dakotans will raise the question of bison.
Point of order, the New Jersey delegation will propose
an amendment to substitute a horse. An armadillo.

A golden bear. A badger or a ruffed grouse.
The Arizona delegation will move to see his papers.
Then some tired soul from the back bench: *I yield my time*

*to the gentleman from Virginia & the lady from Oregon.*
You: *Behold the moose.* Me: A deep curtsy, knee to the floor.
*Yes, behold. Nunc dimittis, Domine.* My work is done.

# Citizen, Poet

Then arose an unseasonable noxious wind,
leaving me tongue-split & sniffing for lightning,
blown sideways into the lampblack of a Congress

of Crows. They, circling deep & widdershins,
scolding & vowel-less, coughing forth (the original)
*Hail to the Chief.* Me, tattered but proud

in a crown of grape withies & chewing gum foil,
clinging to my pocket copy of the Bill of Rights
and mouthing certain glittery words

*(stand beside her*
*and guide her*
*through the night with the light from above)*—

I was quick to learn. None of my kind can suss out
the signs. Though these things I know for sure: right warning
shocks like aluminum across the tongue. The price of tobacco

remains ever stable. Lilacs & camellias trade for little
but soothe the mind of a lonely traveler. Alder whispers
its name. Or warbles it for money. Here, there are few visitors

to the Gallery of Famous Poets & Botanists, but still I mistook
this prayerless and tar-winged land for a nation-state,
for an empire, for a kingdom. And I would have accepted

any appointment—serf or subject, peasant or scold.
But the paper-skinned oracle would have none of it.
Here, even minor cabinet ministers stand for election—

Election Day breaks ravishing. The bald cypress shakes free
its needles and spits its most favored word: *libertine*.
The crows trade cigarettes and tear through the trees

scattering prayer candles & Sacagawea dollars. As for me,
if elected, I will peel back the black earth and lay bare
what is scratched there: *Poet, liar, citizen of the unconscious.*

And yet, with all the ancient liberties and free customs,
the ballots are burned with aplomb. The wind dies down,
and it's unanimous. I am expelled with a hacksaw, a faint

salute, a nosegay of orange nasturtium & wilting
honeysuckle. On the surface, the old streets wind bright
and unmappable. I cannot measure the length

of the hours or recall the name of each ashen face.
Pliny the Elder turns out to be unreliable.
Crows do not speak with a split tongue, and wine

is rife with lies. The shadow of bruised black feathers
cast long in the mind of the returned. I cannot flirt the comforts
now. No. But I will carry this dark cinder for the nation.

# NOTES & COMMONPLACES

## Dear DAR, An Essay

"Any woman 18 years or older, regardless of race, religion, or ethnic background, who can prove lineal descent from a patriot of the American Revolution, is eligible for membership" in the Daughters of the American Revolution.

## On First Encountering Lightning Bugs at the Tidal Basin

On April 13, 1943—Thomas Jefferson's 200th birthday—President Franklin Delano Roosevelt laid the cornerstone of Jefferson Memorial in the site of what had been a "whites only" beach on the Tidal Basin in Washington, D.C.

## Doctrine of Discovery

To the garden the world anew ascending,
Potent mates, daughters, sons, preluding,
The love, the life of their bodies, meaning and being,
Curious here behold my resurrection after slumber
      —Walt Whitman, *Children of Adam*

≈

In 1823, in an opinion authored by Chief Justice John Marshall, the Supreme Court decided *Johnson v. M'Intosh*, concluding that the United States had derived its right of dominion over unoccupied land from

England, the Christian empire that had discovered it. By way of *Johnson* and the decisions that followed, the tribes became tenants on lands they had lived on for millennia.

~

Thomas Jefferson was born on his father's plantation—Shadwell—on April 13, 1743.

~

"As to Spanish, it was so easy that [Jefferson] had learned it, with the help of a Don Quixote lent him by Mr. Cabot, and a grammar, in the course of a passage to Europe, on which he was but nineteen days at sea. But Mr. Jefferson tells large stories..."
        —John Adams Journal Entry November 1804.

~

*Melungeon* is a term traditionally applied to members of one of the tri-racial isolates in the Southeastern United States.

~

"Kindly separated by nature and a wide ocean from the exterminating havoc of one quarter of the globe; too high minded to endure the degradations of the others, possessing a chosen country, with room enough for our descendants to the thousandth and thousandth generation, entertaining a due sense of our equal right to the use of our own faculties, to the acquisitions of our own industry, to honor and confidence from our fellow citizens, resulting not from birth, but from our actions and their sense of them, enlightened by a benign religion, professed indeed and practised in various forms, yet all of them inculcating honesty, truth, temperance, gratitude and the love of man, acknowledging and adoring an overruling providence, which by all its dispensations proves that it delights in the happiness of man here, and his greater happiness hereafter; with all these blessings, what more is necessary to make us a happy and a prosperous people?"

—Thomas Jefferson, First Inaugural, March 4, 1801

～

"But as it is, we have the wolf by the ear, and we can neither hold him, nor safely let him go. Justice is in one scale, and self-preservation in the other."

—Thomas Jefferson to John Holmes, April 22, 1820 (on the question of slavery)

～

"About 10 chosen woodsmen headed by Capt. Lewis my secretary will set out on it immediately & probably accomplish it in two seasons. Capt. Lewis is brave, prudent, habituated to the woods, & familiar with Indian manners and character."

—Thomas Jefferson to Benjamin Rush, February 28, 1803

～

At Monticello, the Jefferson daughters and granddaughters referred to housekeeping as "carrying the keys."

～

"Can one generation bind another, and all others, in succession forever? I think not. The Creator has made the earth for the living, not the dead. Rights and powers can only belong to persons, not to things, not to mere matter, unendowed with will. The dead are not even things. The particles of matter which composed their bodies, make part now of the bodies of other animals, vegetables, or minerals, of a thousand forms. To what then are attached the rights and powers they held while in the form of men? . . . .Nothing then is unchangeable but the inherent and unalienable rights of man."

—Thomas Jefferson to Major John Cartwright, June 5, 1824

~

The backbone of deoxyribonucleic acid (DNA) is based on a repeated pattern of a deoxyribose sugar group and phosphate.

## ARS DEMOCRACIA

"The executive Power shall be vested in a President of the United States of America."
—Constitution of the United States, Article II, Section 1, Clause 1

## ARROWS OF DESIRE: A MELANCHOLY

Bring me my Bow of burning gold;
Bring me my Arrows of desire:
Bring me my Spear: O clouds unfold!
Bring me my Chariot of fire!

I will not cease from Mental Fight,
Nor shall my Sword sleep in my hand:
Till we have built Jerusalem,
In England's green & pleasant Land
—William Blake

## COMPULSORY EDUCATION

The Willamette Meteorite, originally found in Clackamas County, Oregon, was long held sacred by the tribes of Western Oregon. In 2001, the Confederated

Tribes of Grande Ronde settled a lawsuit with the American Museum of Natural History, allowing tribal members to come once a year to conduct a private ceremony.

## Writ of Habeas Corpus

"The privilege of the Writ of Habeas Corpus shall not be suspended, unless when in Cases of Rebellion or Invasion the public Safety may require it."
— Constitution of the United States, Article I, Section 9.

## A Letter on the Matter of an Elk for Monticello

In planning the grove at Monticello, Thomas Jefferson made notes of his plans to "procure a buck-elk, to be, as it were, monarch of the wood; but keep him shy, that his appearance may not lose its effect by too much familiarity."

∽

Patrick Gass, a sergeant and carpenter on the Lewis and Clark Expedition, reported that the Corps killed 131 elk in the winter they spent at Fort Clatsop, near the mouth of the Columbia.

∽

"The settler and pioneer have at bottom had justice on their side; this great continent could not have been kept as nothing but a game preserve for squalid savages."
— Theodore Roosevelt, *The Winning of the West (1889–1896)*

## Saturday Night at Mary Todd's Workers Bar & Grill

"I seem to be the scape-goat for both North and South."
    —Mary Todd Lincoln

## The Ink & Needle of a Compass Rose

In the summer of 1785, Jefferson met John Ledyard, a young British adventurer who had been with Captain Cook on his final, ill-fated voyage to Hawaii. In 1787, TJ proposed that Ledyard walk from Siberia to Alaska and then across North America to Virginia. Because Ledyard could not carry scientific instruments through Russia without arousing suspicion, TJ suggested that he tattoo the measure of an English foot on his arm and then determine latitude with two sticks and a circle drawn in the dirt. TJ also suggested that Ledyard record his location and findings on his own skin with tattoos made from berry juice.

≈

Ledyard started across Russia but was arrested in Siberia by the forces of Catherine the Great in February 1788.

≈

Portland, Oregon:  45.5236° N, 122.6750° W

≈

"Liberty is to faction what air is to fire, an aliment without which it instantly expires. But it could not be less folly to abolish liberty, which is essential to political life, because it nourishes faction, than it would be to wish the annihilation of air, which is essential to animal life, because it imparts to fire its destructive agency."
    —*from* Federalist 10.

~

"And what I assume you shall assume,
For every atom belonging to me as good belongs to you."
    —Walt Whitman, "Song of Myself"

~

The Columbia River Bar, where the river runs into the Pacific is three miles wide and six miles long. Since 1792, approximately 2,000 large ships have sunk in and around the Columbia Bar, earning it its name "the Graveyard of the Pacific."

## A LONG-LATE PLEDGE

Francis Bellamy first wrote the Pledge of Allegiance in 1892, and it was formally adopted by Congress in 1942. The Pledge has been modified four times, most notably adding "Under God" by Joint Congressional Resolution on Flag Day 1954.

~

Abraham Lincoln delivered the Gettysburg Address on Thursday, November 19, 1863. It was 268 words long and took just over two minutes to deliver.

~

"Ocian in view! O! the joy!"
    —Captain William Clark, November 7, 1805

# MORE NOTES ON THE THEORY OF AMERICAN DEGENERACY

Thomas Jefferson spent several years during the Revolutionary War and just after working to disprove the "theory of degeneracy," which was being advanced by the French scientist, Count Georges-Louis Leclerc Buffon, among others. To disprove the theory that the animals and people of the New World were weak and feeble from living in a damp and pernicious climate, TJ conceived and executed a madcap expedition to have a stuffed American moose delivered to the Count in his Paris salon.

◇

"Where shall I learn to get my peace again?
To banish thoughts of that most hateful land,
Dungeoner of my friends, that wicked strand
Where they were wreck'd and live a wrecked life;
That monstrous region, whose dull rivers pour
Ever from their sordid urns unto the shore,
Unown'd of any weedy-haired gods;
Whose winds, all zephyrless, hold scourging rods,
Iced in the great lakes, to afflict mankind"
        —John Keats, "Lines to Fanny"

◇

*Nunc dimittis servum tuum, Domine*:  Now thou dost dismiss thy servant, O Lord

"Lord, now lettest though thy servant depart in peace. . ."
        —Luke 2:29.

◇

"Dear General,

—The apology in your letter of the 8th inst for not calling on me in your passage thro' our nbhood was quite unnecessary. The motions of a traveller are always controuled by so many imperious circumstances that wishes and courtesies must yield to their sway. It was reported among us, on I know not what authority, that you would be in Charlsvl on the 1st inst, on your way to Congress. I went there to have the pleasure of paying you my respects, but after staying some hours, met with a person lately from Staunton who assured me you had passed that place & gone on by the way of Winchester. I comforted myself then with the French adage that what is delayed is not therefore lost; and certainly in your passages to & from Washington should your travelling convenience ever permit a deviation to Monto. I shall receive you with distinguished welcome. Perhaps our University which you visited in it's unfinished state when finished & furnished with it's scientific popln, may tempt you to make a little stay with us. This will probably be by the close of the ensuing year, when it may appear to you worthy of encouraging the youth of your quarter as well as others to seek there the finishing complement of their education. I flatter myself it will assume a standing secondary to nothing in our country. If I live to see this I shall sing with cheerfulness the song of old Simeon's *nunc dimittis Domine. . .*"

—Thomas Jefferson to General Andrew Jackson, December 18, 1823

## CITIZEN, POET

"And the city of London shall have all its ancient liberties and free customs, as well by land as by water; furthermore, we decree and grant that all other cities, boroughs, towns, and ports shall have all their liberties and free customs."

—The Magna Carta, Chapter 13

## ACKNOWLEDGMENTS & GRATITUDES

Many many thanks to those who have read this book in its various forms, including Lia Purpura, Greg Glazner, Kevin Clark, Kathleen Halme, and (of course) David Biespiel. And a bottomless well of gratitude to my dear ones, Ruby, Violet, Luke, and David.

*Mud Season Review*:  "Stitch: The Forest"; "One Saturday Night at Mary Todd's Workers Bar & Grill"; "Bear Hungry"; "Writ of Habeas Corpus"

*The Oregonian*:  "More Notes on the Theory of American Degeneracy" reprinted in *Poems of the American South*

*Windfall*: "They Say It Makes Us Strong to Swim Before Winter's End "

*ZYZZYVA*: "Stitch: A Warning"